Welcome to the exciting world of tennis through the pages of "The 50 Legends of Tennis and Their Stories". This book takes you to the legendary courts, to the epic matches and moments that have shaped this iconic sport.

From Björn Borg to Serena Williams, Rod Laver to Naomi Osaka, each name evokes an era, a technique and a passion.

Get ready to explore the dazzling backhands, unstoppable serves and memorable exchanges that have marked the history of tennis. Each story immerses you in the intensity of the competition, the adrenalin of the finals and the perseverance of the players who reached the top.

Through these legends, discover how tennis has become much more than just a game, but a true global passion.

SUMMARY

- #1- ROGER FEDERER
- #2- RAFAEL NADAL
- #3- NOVAK DJOKOVIC
- #4- ROD LAVER
- #5- BJORN BORG
- #6- PETE SAMPRAS
- #7- ANDRE AGASSI
- #8- JOHN MCENROE
- #9- JIMMY CONNORS
- #10- IVAN LENDL
- #11- ARTHUR ASHE
- #12- STEFAN EDBERG
- #13- BORIS BECKER
- #14- KEN ROSEWALL
- #15- PANCHO GONZALES
- #16- DON BUDGE
- #17- BILL TILDEN
- #18- ROY EMERSON
- #19- JACK KRAMER
- #20- FRED PERRY
- #21- RENE LACOSTE
- #22- SERENA WILLIAMS
- #23- GUILLERMO VILAS
- #24- STAN SMITH
- #25- GUSTAVO KUERTEN

SUMMARY

#26- YANNICK NOAH
#27- ILIE NASTASE
#28- JOHN NEWCOMBE
#29- TONY TRABERT
#30- MARIA SHARAPOVA
#31- PANCHO SEGURA
#32- MANUEL SANTANA
#33- JIM COURIER
#34- PATRICK RAFTER
#35- THOMAS MUSTER
#36- LLEYTON HEWITT
#37- ANDY RODDICK
#38- TONY ROCHE
#39- FRED STOLLE
#40- JACK CRAWFORD
#41- BILLIE JEAN KING
#42- MONICA SELES
#43- DAVID NALBANDIAN
#44- MARTINA NAVRATILOVA
#45- VENUS WILLIAMS
#46- ROY EMERSON
#47- STEFFI GRAF
#48- MARGARET COURT
#49- LEW HOAD
#50- CHRIS EVERT

#1

ROGER FEDERER

BORN AUGUST 8, 1981 IN BASEL, SWITZERLAND

With 20 Grand Slam titles to his name, Roger Federer has dominated the tennis world like few have. His victories include 8 Wimbledon, 6 Australian Open, 5 US Open and 1 French Open. His mastery of the game, his grace on the court and his fair play off the court have earned him worldwide admiration.

ELEGANCE AND SUSTAINABILITY INCARNATE

What makes Federer famous, beyond his titles, is his timeless elegance, his ability to stay at the top of the game for two decades, and his fluid style of play that seems to defy the ages. He is recognized for his formidable forehand, his exceptional footwork, and an unparalleled tactical sense. His rivalries with Nadal and Djokovic also made history, providing some of the sport's most memorable matches.

Federer marked tennis with moments of excellence and emotion. His first Grand Slam at Wimbledon in 2003 heralded an era of domination. His fight to return to the top after injuries and at an age when many retire is a testament to his determination and love for the game. His victory at the 2017 Australian Open, after a six-month break due to injury, at the age of 35, is particularly remarkable. Off the court, his philanthropic commitment through the Roger Federer Foundation, which supports the education of children in Africa and Switzerland, highlights his impact beyond tennis.

Declared unfit for military service, he was directed to civil protection in 2003 but could not attend classes because of his schedule.

#2

RAFAEL NADAL, "RAFA"

BORN JUNE 3, 1986 IN MANACOR, ON THE ISLAND OF MAJORCA, SPAIN.

With 22 Grand Slam titles, Rafael Nadal holds the record in this category, surpassing even legends like Roger Federer and Novak Djokovic. His impressive collection includes 14 titles at Roland Garros, an all-time record, 2 at Wimbledon, 4 at the US Open and 2 at the Australian Open.

CLAY AS A KINGDOM

Nadal is famous for his incomparable success on clay, a surface where he has dominated like no other. His ability to play powerful and precise shots, combined with exceptional endurance, makes him a formidable opponent. His matches against Federer, including their epic showdown at Wimbledon in 2008, have gone down in history. Nadal is also known for his perseverance in the face of injuries, always coming back stronger, defying expectations and age limits.

Nadal left an indelible mark in the history of tennis with his victories and his competitive spirit. His first French Open title in 2005, at the age of 19, was the start of an era of dominance on clay. His clashes with Federer and Djokovic are legendary moments, raising the level of the game. His ability to come back from serious injuries, notably his recurring knee problems, and maintain a high level of play is a testament to his mental and physical strength. Off the court, his commitment to various charitable causes and his humble and respectful attitude make him a role model for many.

In 1998, he won the Auray Super 12 Open, while he was still hesitating between football and tennis. This is the date that Rafael Nadal says today that he started his career

#3

NOVAK DJOKOVIC

BORN MAY 22, 1987 IN BELGRADE, SERBIA.

With 20 Grand Slam titles, Novak Djokovic is tied with Roger Federer and just behind Rafael Nadal. His record includes 9 Australian Opens, 6 Wimbledons, 3 US Opens and 2 Roland-Garros. Djokovic also stands out for his dominant presence at the top of the ATP rankings, holding the record for the number of weeks as world number 1.

DJOKOVIC'S ASCENSION

Novak Djokovic is famous for his remarkable ability to dominate in the most difficult situations. His incredible mental resilience, discipline, and ability to adapt to all opponents and surfaces sets him apart. His rivalries with Federer and Nadal resulted in some of the most memorable matches in tennis history, including the 2019 Wimbledon final against Federer, one of the longest and most dramatic in history.

Djokovic's career is full of impressive moments. His first Grand Slam victory at the Australian Open in 2008 marked the start of his rise. His 2011 season remains one of the most impressive in tennis history, with three Grand Slam titles and five Masters 1000s. The way he overcame injuries and controversies, to come back ever stronger, is a testament to his strength Character. Off the court, his humanitarian commitment, notably through his foundation which supports the education of children in Serbia, shows his social involvement.

In June 2023, he won his 23rd Grand Slam title, at Roland Garros, becoming the sole male record holder and the oldest player to have won this tournament at 36 years and 20 days.

#4

ROD LAVER, "ROCKET"

BORN AUGUST 9, 1938 IN ROCKHAMPTON, QUEENSLAND, AUSTRALIA.

Rod Laver holds the impressive record of two career Grand Slams, achieved in 1962 and 1969, a feat unmatched to this day. Laver has won a total of 11 Grand Slam titles, including four times each at Wimbledon and the Australian Open, as well as the US Open twice and the French Open once.

THE MAN WITH TWO GRAND SLAMS

Rod Laver is famous for being the only player in tennis history to win the singles Grand Slam, in both the Amateur and Open eras. What makes him unique is his exceptional versatility and his dominance in an important period of transition for tennis. Laver was known for his aggressive play, impeccable technique and great left-handed skill. His revolutionary victories not only marked the history of the sport but also contributed to the popularization of tennis across the world.

Laver's career has been punctuated with historic moments. His first Grand Slam in 1962 established him as an elite player, but it was his 1969 Grand Slam that really stood out, achieved after the move to professionalism. This double feat is a testament to his ability to adapt and excel despite major changes in the sport. Laver also played a key role in promoting professional tennis, participating in matches and tournaments that paved the way for the Open era. Off the court, his simplicity and integrity have made him a role model for many players.

The honors bestowed upon him are numerous: he was inducted into the International Tennis Hall of Fame in 1981, the Australian Open renamed its center court Rod Laver Arena in 2001, the Laver Cup owes its name to him and he is appeared in a series of Australian legends postage stamps in 2003.

#5

BJORN BORG, "ICEBORG"

BORN JUNE 6, 1956 IN STOCKHOLM, SWEDEN.

Bjorn Borg won 11 Grand Slam titles, including five consecutive victories at Wimbledon (1976-1980) and six at Roland Garros (1974-1975, 1978-1981). His dominance on grass and clay was unprecedented at the time. Borg retired from high-level tennis at the age of just 26.

THE BORG MYSTERY

Bjorn Borg is famous for his ability to remain calm under pressure, earning him the nickname "Ice Man." His style of play, characterized by a strong baseline and powerful shots, was ahead of its time. Borg also left his mark on tennis through his rivalry with John McEnroe, notably during their epic confrontation at Wimbledon in 1980, considered one of the greatest tennis matches of all time.

Borg's career is littered with memorable moments. His winning streak at Wimbledon and Roland Garros set records that are difficult to beat. His duels with McEnroe, particularly the 1980 Wimbledon final, offered a contrast of styles and personalities that captivated the tennis world. Off the court, his impact on the popularity of tennis in Europe and his contribution to sports fashion, notably with his Fila headbands and polo shirts, have been significant. Borg's early retirement left his fans and the tennis world searching for answers, adding to his mystery and legendary status.

In 2005, American journalists from Tennis Magazine placed him 5th among "the forty greatest tennis champions of the last forty years". He was entered into the International Tennis Hall of Fame in 1987.

#6

PETE SAMPRAS, "PISTOL PETE"

BORN ON AUGUST 12, 1971 IN WASHINGTON D.C., UNITED STATES.

Pete Sampras won 14 Grand Slam titles, a record in his time, including seven titles at Wimbledon, five at the US Open, and two at the Australian Open. Renowned for his serving and volleying, Sampras dominated men's tennis in the 1990s, finishing six consecutive years as world number 1.

THE ART OF SERVICE

Pete Sampras is famous for revolutionizing the serve-and-volley game. His ability to dominate points with his serve, considered one of the best of all time, redefined strategies in tennis. His rivalry with Andre Agassi, which provided a stark contrast between Sampras' serve-and-volley style and Agassi's baseline game, marked the 90s.

Sampras' career is marked by key moments. His seven titles at Wimbledon between 1993 and 2000 testify to his domination on grass. His last Grand Slam victory at the US Open in 2002, where he beat long-time rival Agassi, is an iconic moment, concluding his career on a triumphant note. Off the court, Sampras is known for his discretion and professionalism, remaining out of the spotlight despite his fame. His influence on the game and future generations of players is undeniable, with many taking inspiration from his style and work ethic.

In 2007, Sampras returned to the tennis courts by participating in senior circuit tournaments. On May 6, 2007, he won the Boston tournament against Todd Martin in 3 sets (6-3, 5-7, 11-9).

#7

ANDRE AGASSI, "THE PUNISHER"

BORN APRIL 29, 1970 IN LAS VEGAS, NEVADA, UNITED STATES.

With 8 Grand Slam titles to his credit, his record is remarkable: 4 Australian Opens, 2 US Opens, 1 Wimbledon, and 1 Roland-Garros. Andre Agassi is one of the rare players to have achieved the Career Grand Slam. Agassi was also ranked number 1 in the world, and won the gold medal at the 1996 Olympic Games in Atlanta.

THE REBEL AND REDEEMER TENNIS ICON

Andre Agassi is famous for his explosive style of play, his unique look, and his ability to come back to the top after tough times. Known for his powerful and precise baseline game, he revolutionized tennis with his formidable returns of serve. His rivalry with Pete Sampras was one of the greatest in tennis history, pitting two distinct styles and personalities against each other.

Agassi's career is punctuated by remarkable highs and lows. His first Grand Slam at Wimbledon in 1992 established his reputation as an exceptional player. His fall in the rankings in the mid-90s, followed by a spectacular comeback to become world number 1 in 1999, is a story of resilience and determination. His involvement in charitable causes, including the Andre Agassi Foundation for Education, has had a significant impact off the court. His rivalry with Sampras, culminating in their confrontation at the 2001 US Open, remains a defining moment in tennis.

At the age of nine, he played a match against American football player Jim Brown (then 43) who bet $500. Agassi won the match 6-3, 6-3, 6-2.

#8

JOHN MCENROE, "MAC"

BORN FEBRUARY 16, 1959 IN WIESBADEN, WEST GERMANY

John McEnroe won 7 Grand Slam singles titles: 3 at Wimbledon (1981, 1983, 1984) and 4 at the US Open (1979, 1980, 1981, 1984). McEnroe also dominated in doubles, winning 9 Grand Slam titles in this category. He finished four years (1981-1984) as world number 1 in singles.

STORM ON THE COURT

John McEnroe is famous not only for his genius on the court, but also for his volcanic temper and his confrontations with referees. His style of play, characterized by impeccable technique and tactical intelligence, stood in stark contrast to his often controversial behavior. His rivalry with Bjorn Borg, culminating in the 1980 Wimbledon final, remains one of the greatest in tennis history.

McEnroe's career is full of notable events. His victory at the US Open in 1979, at just 20 years old, launched his career. His rivalry with Borg, particularly their epic showdown at Wimbledon in 1980, has become the stuff of legend. Off the court, his escapades and outbursts against officials often made headlines, sometimes overshadowing his tennis prowess. After his career, McEnroe became a respected commentator, bringing his expertise and uniqueness to tennis broadcasting.

This strong personality caused him to be excluded from the 1990 Australian Open, during his round of 16 match 6-1, 4-6, 7-5, 2-4 against Mikael Pernfors. In this match, McEnroe successively taunted a linesman, broke a racket and insulted the central referee.

#9

JIMMY CONNORS, "JIMBO"

BORN SEPTEMBER 2, 1952 IN EAST SAINT LOUIS, UNITED STATES.

Jimmy Connors is an iconic tennis figure, famous for his longevity and fighting spirit. He has won 8 Grand Slam titles, including 5 US Opens (a record for a man), 2 Wimbledons, and 1 Australian Open. Connors was also world number 1 for 268 weeks, a record at the time.

COMBATIVENESS INCARNATE

Jimmy Connors is famous for his fighting spirit and "warrior" attitude on the court. His baseline game, his consistency, and his famous two-handed backhand were his trademark. Connors was known for his explosive temperament and ability to captivate crowds, often playing the role of the underdog. His rivalry with John McEnroe and Bjorn Borg contributed to one of the most competitive and entertaining periods in tennis history.

Connors' career is full of memorable moments. His 1974 US Open title, where he beat Ken Rosewall, was a key moment, as was his 1974 Wimbledon victory over McEnroe. Connors is also known for his remarkable appearances at the US Open, where he reached the semi-finals at age 39 in 1991, captivating audiences with his fighting spirit. His uncompromising approach to the game, his longevity and his continued success in an ever-changing sport are testament to his talent and determination.

One of his flagship records, certainly one of the most underestimated and yet one of the most significant, is his presence in the Top 3 of the world rankings at the end of the singles season, for 12 consecutive years (from 1973 to 1984). .

#10

IVAN LENDL

BORN MARCH 7, 1960 IN OSTRAVA, CZECHOSLOVAKIA

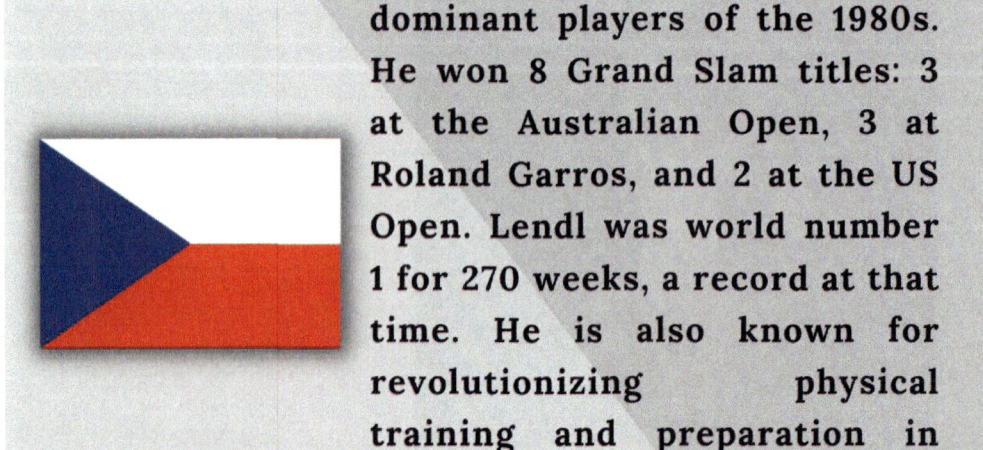

Ivan Lendl is one of the most dominant players of the 1980s. He won 8 Grand Slam titles: 3 at the Australian Open, 3 at Roland Garros, and 2 at the US Open. Lendl was world number 1 for 270 weeks, a record at that time. He is also known for revolutionizing physical training and preparation in tennis.

THE INNOVATOR OF MODERN TENNIS

Ivan Lendl is famous for transforming professional tennis through his methodical approach and commitment to fitness. His ability to maintain a high level of performance throughout the year has changed the way players approach the tour. His rivalry with players like McEnroe, Connors and Wilander resulted in some memorable matches. Lendl is also recognized for his powerful baseline game, particularly his forehand, and for being one of the first to use topspin effectively.

Lendl's career is marked by impressive achievements. His consecutive victories at the French Open (1986, 1987) and the US Open (1985, 1986, 1987) established his reputation as an uncompromising and resilient player. His move from Czechoslovakia to the United States was also a key moment, reflecting the political changes of the time. Off the court, his impact on coaching modernization and successful transition into the coaching role influenced future generations of players.

Best player in the history of Czech tennis, Ivan Lendl has been a member of the International Tennis Hall of Fame since 2001.

#11

ARTHUR ASHE

BORN JULY 10, 1943 IN RICHMOND, UNITED STATES

Arthur Ashe remains one of the most influential players in tennis history, not only for his achievements on the court, but also for his impact off it. He won three Grand Slam singles titles: the US Open in 1968, the Australian Open in 1970 and Wimbledon in 1975. Ashe was the first black player selected for the United States Davis Cup team.

PIONEER ON AND OFF THE COURT

Arthur Ashe is famous for breaking racial barriers in tennis. He used his fame to fight against segregation and apartheid, making him a leading figure in the civil rights movement. On the court, his triumph at Wimbledon in 1975 against Jimmy Connors remains one of the most memorable moments in tennis history. Off the court, he has been a staunch advocate for human rights and education, helping to raise awareness of HIV/AIDS after revealing his own illness.

Ashe marked tennis with many firsts: first African American selected for the United States Davis Cup team, first to win the US Open, and first to win Wimbledon. His victory at Wimbledon against Connors, one of the favorites, was a demonstration of tactics and calm under pressure. Off the court, Ashe has been an educator and humanitarian, writing books and lecturing on social and health issues. He died in 1993, but his legacy continues to inspire.

The center court at the USTA National Tennis Center at Flushing Meadows (where the US Open is played) has been named after him since its creation in 1997.

#12

STEFAN EDBERG

BORN ON JANUARY 19, 1966 IN VÄSTERVIK, SWEDEN.

Stefan Edberg has won 6 Grand Slam singles titles: two Wimbledons (1988, 1990), two US Opens (1991, 1992) and two Australian Opens (1985, 1987). Edberg was also famous for his elegant serve-and-volley game, a technique that has become less common in modern tennis. He finished two years (1990 and 1991) as world number 1.

THE ELEGANCE OF SERVE AND VOLLEY

Stefan Edberg is famous for his elegant style of play and his mastery of the serve and volley, a technique he has taken to an art level. His ability to combine power and precision in his serves, followed by incisive volleys, has made him one of the most feared players on grass and hard courts. His rivalry with Boris Becker, particularly at Wimbledon, resulted in some classic tennis matches.

Edberg's career is peppered with memorable moments. His victories at Wimbledon against Becker are particularly notable, demonstrating his mastery of the grass court game. His ability to stay at the top of the game for several years, in an era dominated by players like Becker and Sampras, is a testament to his quality and consistency. Off the court, Edberg is recognized for his involvement in charity work and his role as a role model for young players, promoting sport and fair play.

Stefan Edberg founded a tennis school in Vaxjö with Mats Wilander. He is also one of Adidas' global ambassadors.

#13

BORIS BECKER, "BOOM BOOM"

BORN NOVEMBER 22, 1967 IN LEIMEN, WEST GERMANY

Boris Becker won 6 Grand Slam titles, including three at Wimbledon (1985, 1986, 1989), two at the Australian Open (1991, 1996) and one at the US Open (1989). Becker is particularly famous for winning Wimbledon at the age of 17, becoming the youngest champion at that tournament.

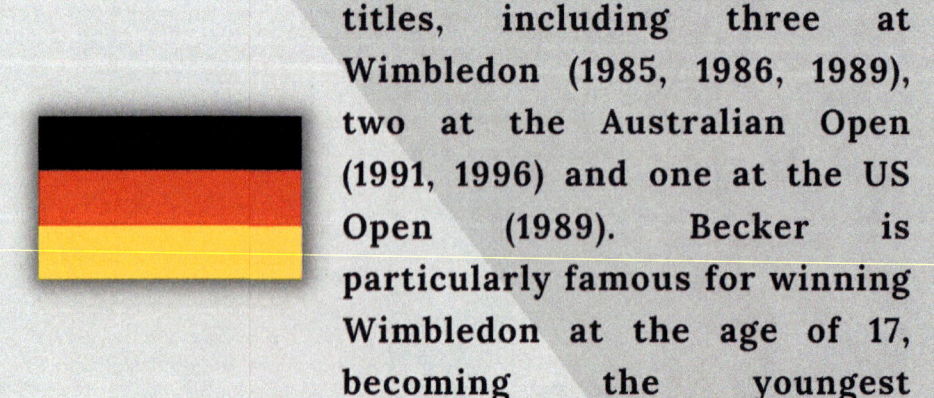

LIGHTNING FROM LEIMEN

Boris Becker is famous for his explosive style of play and his charisma on the court. His serve and volley, among the best in tennis history, combined with his combative temperament, made him a fan favorite. His victory at Wimbledon at age 17 shook the tennis world and set a new standard for young players. His rivalry with Stefan Edberg, notably during their clashes at Wimbledon, marked a golden era of tennis.

Becker's career is full of significant moments. In addition to his early victory at Wimbledon, his duels with Edberg and Agassi remain fondly remembered. His ability to excel on all surfaces, winning major titles on grass, hard and indoor, demonstrates his versatility. Off the court, Becker became known for his philanthropic activities and his time in the media as a commentator and coach, continuing to influence the world of tennis.

In 2022, he was found guilty of four counts related to his personal bankruptcy, and was imprisoned. He is one of those tennis champions, like Björn Borg or Vitas Gerulaitis, having experienced quite complicated, even tormented, "post-tennis" years.

#14

KEN ROSEWALL, "MUSCLES"

BORN NOVEMBER 2, 1934 IN SYDNEY, AUSTRALIA.

Ken Rosewall is one of the great champions of the pre-Open and early Open eras of tennis. He has won 8 Grand Slam singles titles: 4 at the Australian Open, 2 at Roland Garros and 2 at the US Open. Rosewall is notable for his longevity in the sport, having won major titles over a period of almost two decades.

THE LONGEVITY OF ROSEWALL

Ken Rosewall is famous for his exceptional longevity and elegance on the court. His ability to remain competitive at a high level well beyond the age where most players retire is a testament to his physical fitness and commitment to the game. His graceful style of play, combining speed, finesse and strategy, distinguished him from his more powerful contemporaries. He also played a key role in the transition from amateur tennis to professionalism.

Rosewall's career is punctuated with memorable moments. His victory at the US Open in 1970 at the age of 35 and his final at Wimbledon in 1974 at the age of 39 illustrate his remarkable ability to compete with younger players. Rosewall was also a pioneer in the professional game, playing a key role in tours like those of Jack Kramer, which helped shape modern professional tennis. Off the court, he is known for his gentlemanliness and fair play, characteristics which have greatly contributed to his tennis legacy.

Rosewall is the player who has probably played the most singles in the history of men's tennis, at least 2,282 known to date.

#15

PANCHO GONZALES, "PANCHO"

BORN MAY 9, 1928 IN LOS ANGELES, CALIFORNIA, UNITED STATES.

Pancho Gonzales is one of the most influential players of the pre-Open era of tennis. He won 2 Grand Slam singles titles, both at the US Open, in 1948 and 1949. His career spanned several decades, during which he dominated the professional circuit, winning a large number of titles.

THE TITAN OF PROFESSIONAL TENNIS

Pancho Gonzales is famous for his incredible serve, considered one of the best in tennis history. His aggressive style of play and passionate on-court temperament have made him an iconic figure. Gonzales played a key role in popularizing professional tennis, participating in tours and matches that set the stage for the Open era.

Gonzales' career was marked by legendary rivalries and unforgettable matches. His dominance on the professional circuit in the 1950s and 1960s set high standards for future generations. He is best known for his marathon matches, notably against Charlie Pasarell at Wimbledon in 1969, which lasted more than 5 hours. Off the court, his journey from humble beginnings to becoming a tennis legend is an inspiration. Gonzales also played an important role in the fight for recognition and fair compensation for professional players.

Gonzales was married six times (twice to actress Madelyn Darrow) and had seven children.

#16

DONALD BUDGE

BORN JUNE 13, 1915 IN OAKLAND, CALIFORNIA, UNITED STATES.

Donald Budge is a legendary figure in tennis history, primarily for being the first player to achieve the Grand Slam in 1938. He won a total of 6 Grand Slam singles titles, including all four majors in 1938 - the Australian Open, Roland-Garros, Wimbledon and the US Open.

GRAND SLAM PIONEER

Donald Budge is famous for establishing one of the greatest feats in tennis: the Grand Slam in 1938. His achievement set a standard of excellence and became a prestigious goal for tennis players. Aside from his Grand Slam, Budge was known for his all-around style of play, mastering both the technical and tactical aspects of the game. His dominance in the 1930s laid the foundation for modern tennis and greatly influenced future generations of players.

Budge's career was marked by historic moments, including his Grand Slam in 1938. He also played a major role in international competitions, helping the American team win the Davis Cup on several occasions. His rivalry with other great players of the era, such as Fred Perry and Ellsworth Vines, was a highlight of his career. Unfortunately, his career was cut short by World War II, which limited his opportunities to win further major titles.

In December 1999, he suffered a car accident from which he did not recover and died the following month.

#17

BILL TILDEN, "BIG BILL"

BORN FEBRUARY 10, 1893 IN PHILADELPHIA, PENNSYLVANIA, UNITED STATES.

Bill Tilden is one of the greatest tennis players in history and an iconic figure of the 1920s and 1930s. He won 10 Grand Slam singles titles, including 7 at the US Open (a record that stood for several decades) and 3 at Wimbledon. Tilden has led the U.S. Davis Cup team to victory seven times.

LEGEND OF CENTER COURT

Bill Tilden is famous for his revolutionary impact on tennis. He dominated the sport in the 1920s, bringing a new tactical and technical dimension to the game. His presence on the court, combined with his charisma and flamboyant personality, made him an international star. Tilden was also known for his writings on tennis, helping to teach and promote the game to a wider audience. His influence helped establish tennis as a major sport in the United States.

Tilden's career has been punctuated by many notable moments, including his multiple victories at the US Open and Wimbledon. He was almost unbeatable in the Davis Cup, playing a key role in American victories. His rivalry with other great players of the era, such as René Lacoste and Henri Cochet, was a high point of interwar tennis. Off the court, Tilden has also been a controversial figure, with a personal life that has often attracted media attention.

Tilden has perhaps spent more time analyzing tennis than anyone before or after him. He was the author of two sports books, The Art of Lawn Tennis2 and Match Play and the Spin of the Ball.

#18

ROY EMERSON

BORN NOVEMBER 3, 1936 IN BLACKBUTT, QUEENSLAND, AUSTRALIA.

Roy Emerson won 12 singles titles, including 6 Australian Opens, 2 French Opens, 2 Wimbledons and 2 US Opens. In doubles, he added 16 more Grand Slam titles to his record. Emerson is the first player to win a career Grand Slam in both singles and doubles.

THE KING OF GRAND SLAM TITLES

Roy Emerson is famous for his ability to excel in both singles and doubles, a rarity in modern tennis. His game was characterized by his endurance, consistency and intelligent tactics. Emerson was a complete player, able to adapt to all surfaces, which allowed him to win titles on grass, clay and hard courts.

Emerson's career is dotted with remarkable successes, including his multiple victories at the Australian Open, his national tournament. His victories at Wimbledon and the US Open in the 1960s established him as one of the best players of his era. In addition to his tournament success, Emerson is recognized for his commitment to tennis promotion, working to develop the sport in Australia and overseas. His transition to coaching after his playing career also had a significant impact on future generations of Australian players.

He is one of the 8 players in the history of tennis to have won the 4 Grand Slam tournaments.

#19

JACK KRAMER, "BIG JAKE"

BORN AUGUST 1, 1921 IN LAS VEGAS, NEVADA, UNITED STATES.

Jack Kramer is considered one of the most successful tennis players of the 1940s and 1950s. He won 3 Grand Slam singles titles, including 2 at the US Open (1946, 1947) and 1 at Wimbledon (1947).). In doubles, he added 6 Grand Slam titles.

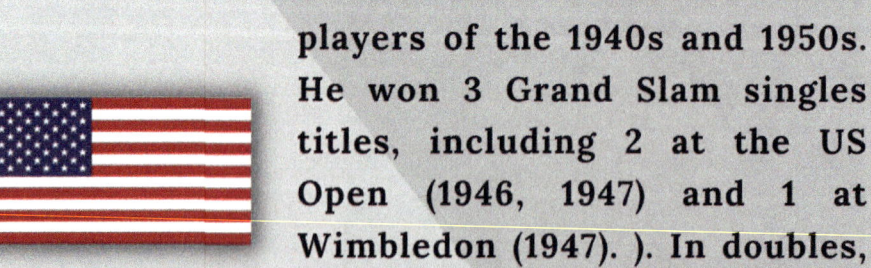

VISIONARY OF MODERN TENNIS

Jack Kramer is famous not only for his on-court prowess, but also for his vision and impact off the court. He was a pioneer in the development of professional tennis, promoting tours and matches that laid the foundation for the Open era. Kramer was known for his powerful serve and volley game, as well as his tactical intelligence. He played a crucial role in the founding of the Association of Tennis Professionals (ATP).

Kramer's career has been marked by significant moments both on and off the court. His victories at the US Open and Wimbledon demonstrated his exceptional talent. However, it was his work as a tennis promoter and administrator that had the most lasting impact, particularly in the fight for players' rights and the establishment of the professional tour. His commitment to tennis transformed the sport, making it more attractive to players and fans.

Actor Bill Pullman plays him in the film Battle of the Sexes, released in 2017.

#20

FRED PERRY

BORN MAY 18, 1909 IN STOCKPORT, ENGLAND.

Fred Perry won 8 Grand Slam singles titles, including 3 consecutive Wimbledons (1934-1936), 3 US Opens (1933, 1934, 1936), 1 Australian Open (1934) and 1 French Open (1935). Perry was the first player to win every career Grand Slam title, a remarkable feat at the time.

PIONEER OF BRITISH TENNIS

Fred Perry is famous for being one of the greatest players in British tennis history, often cited as the best British player of all time. He is best known for breaking social barriers in tennis, a sport traditionally dominated by the British elite. Perry, from a modest background, defied the conventions of his time with his talent and determination.

Perry's career was punctuated by many notable moments, including his back-to-back Wimbledon victories, which cemented his status as a tennis legend. His ability to win titles on all surfaces demonstrated his versatility and mastery of the game. Following his playing career, Perry also left a lasting legacy with the creation of the Fred Perry brand, today synonymous with fashion and British culture.

In the late 1940s, he partnered with Tibby Wegner. Together, they founded the Fred Perry clothing brand. The brand's first polo shirt was created in 1952.

#21

RENE LACOSTE, "THE CROCODILE"

BORN JULY 2, 1904 IN PARIS, FRANCE.

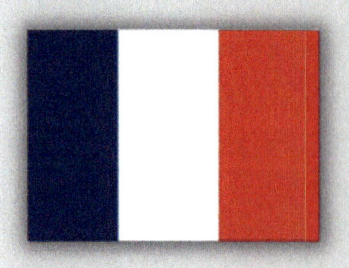

René Lacoste won 7 Grand Slam singles titles: 3 at Roland Garros (1925, 1927, 1929), 2 at Wimbledon (1925, 1928) and 2 at the US Open (1926, 1927). Lacoste was a key member of the "Four Musketeers", a group of French players who dominated world tennis during this period.

THE TENNIS CROCODILE

Nicknamed "The Crocodile" for his tenacity on the court, he was known for his ability to anticipate his opponents' moves and use his intelligence to win points. Lacoste also brought technical innovations to the sport, notably developing the first metal racket and popularizing the wearing of cotton pique shirts, today known under the Lacoste brand.

Lacoste's career was punctuated by important moments, notably his victories at Roland Garros and Wimbledon, which established his reputation on the international stage. His role in France winning the Davis Cup on several occasions was a key moment in the history of French tennis. Off the court, Lacoste's legacy as an innovator in tennis equipment and sports fashion remains a defining aspect of his career.

He was appointed officer of the Legion of Honor in 1977, and honorary president of the FFT. He has also been a member of the International Tennis Hall of Fame since 1976.

#22

SERENA WILLIAMS

BORN SEPTEMBER 26, 1981 IN SAGINAW, MICHIGAN, UNITED STATES.

With 23 Grand Slam singles titles, Serena Williams holds the Open Era record for most singles titles won. His victories include 7 times Wimbledon, 7 times Australian Open, 6 times US Open and 3 times French Open. Serena has also won 14 Grand Slam titles in women's doubles, all with her sister Venus.

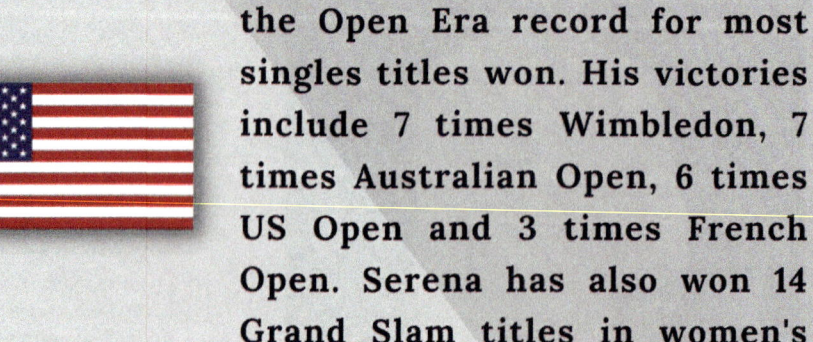

SUPERHUMAN STRENGTH

Serena Williams is famous for her hitting power, speed and ability to dominate the game. Her longevity, her ability to return to the highest level after injury or maternity breaks, is a testament to her resilience and commitment to tennis . Her rivalries with other great players, such as her sister Venus, Maria Sharapova, and more recently Naomi Osaka, have marked the history of women's tennis. Serena is also credited with breaking barriers in a sport traditionally dominated by white athletes.

Serena's career has been marked by historic moments, such as her "Serena Slam" - holding all Grand Slam titles at the same time (but not in the same calendar year). Her victory at the 2017 Australian Open while pregnant was an extraordinary testament to her strength and determination. Off the court, her commitment to social causes, her success in ventures outside of tennis, and her role as a mother have added additional dimensions to her legacy.

Serena Williams is the highest-paid female athlete in the world in 2016, earning over $29 million.

#23

GUILLERMO VILAS, "WILLY"

BORN AUGUST 17 1952 IN BUENOS AIRES, ARGENTINA.

Guillermo Vilas won 4 Grand Slam titles: the Australian Open in 1977 (January and December), French Open in 1977, and the US Open in 1977. Vilas also holds the record for the most titles in a single season, with 16 titles in 1977.

AN ARGENTINE LEGEND ON THE COURTS

Guillermo Vilas is famous for his dominance on clay, a feat symbolized by his victory at the French Open in 1977. He was known for his physical endurance, his ability to play long rallies and his heavy forehand. Vilas was a pioneer of tennis in South America, inspiring a generation of players. His 1977 season remains one of the most remarkable in tennis history, marked by a series of impressive victories and a consistency rarely matched.

Vilas' career was marked by his rivalry with players like Bjorn Borg and Jimmy Connors. His performances in 1977, notably his winning streak and his triumph at Roland Garros, remain key moments in tennis. Off the court, Vilas is recognized for his philosophical approach to the game and his interest in poetry and music. His influence on Argentine and South American tennis is undeniable, making him a true ambassador of the sport.

First Argentine player in history to conquer a Grand Slam tournament,
_____

#24

STAN SMITH, "STAN THE MAN"

BORN DECEMBER 14, 1946 IN PASADENA, CALIFORNIA, UNITED STATES.

Stan Smith won 2 Grand Slam singles titles: the US Open in 1971 and Wimbledon in 1972. Smith also excelled at doubles, winning several Grand Slam titles with partner Bob Lutz. His game was characterized by a powerful serve, excellent volleying, and great precision in his shots.

A LASTING INFLUENCE ON AND OFF THE COURT

Stan Smith is famous not only for his Grand Slam victories, but also for his lasting impact on the world of tennis and beyond. He is one of the first players to have a tennis shoe named in his honor, the famous "Adidas Stan Smith", which has become a timeless fashion symbol. His elegant and efficient game, combined with his professionalism and fair play, made him a role model for future generations of tennis players.

Highlights of Smith's career include his victory at Wimbledon, where he demonstrated his mastery on grass, and his triumph at the US Open. He also played a key role in Team USA's Davis Cup victories. Off the court, Smith has been an ambassador for tennis, helping to popularize the sport through his partnerships and media engagements. His transition into coaching and sports commentary has also enriched the world of tennis.

He gave his name to the Stan Smith shoe for Adidas, shoes that are still popular today. Adidas shoes were officially launched in 1978.

#25

GUSTAVO KUERTEN, "GUGA"

BORN SEPTEMBER 10, 1976 IN FLORIANÓPOLIS, BRAZIL

Gustavo Kuerten is one of the most notable players in tennis in the late 1990s and early 2000s. He won 3 French Open titles (1997, 2000, 2001), making him one of the few players to win several times this prestigious tournament.

THE CHARM OF GUGA ON CLAY

Gustavo Kuerten is famous for his ability to dominate on clay, a surface traditionally dominated by European players. His victory at Roland Garros in 1997 as a little-known and low-ranked player is one of the biggest surprises in tennis history. Guga is also recognized for his charismatic personality and infectious smile, which have earned him great popularity among tennis fans around the world.

Guga's career has been marked by memorable moments, including his three victories at Roland Garros. His meteoric rise in 1997, his emotional victory in 2000 where he drew a heart on the court after his victory, and the successful defense of his title in 2001 remain etched in the memory of tennis fans. Off the court, Guga is known for his involvement in charity work, particularly for underprivileged children in Brazil.

In 2000, he became the first South American player to complete a season at the top of the ATP rankings, a position he held for forty-three weeks.

#26

YANNICK NOAH, "THE CHAMELEON"

BORN MAY 18, 1960 IN SEDAN, FRANCE.

Yannick Noah is recognized as one of the most talented tennis players in France. He won 23 singles titles during his career, the most notable of which was his triumph at Roland-Garros in 1983. This victory made him the last French player to have won the Roland-Garros men's singles tournament at that time. day.

NOAH'S JOY OF LIVING

Yannick Noah is famous for his charismatic personality, his contagious energy on the court and his ability to connect with the public. His victory at Roland Garros in 1983 is historic, not only for its sporting significance, but also because it was celebrated as a moment of national pride in France. Noah is also known for his social and humanitarian commitment, as well as his successful career in music after leaving professional tennis.

In addition to his iconic victory at Roland Garros, Noah has had several notable moments in his career, including his performances in the Davis Cup. He helped France win the Davis Cup in 1991 as team captain, a role he held successfully for several years. His transition to a musical career and his involvement in humanitarian causes have also made an impact, showing his versatility and impact beyond the world of tennis.

Yannick Noah was the first Frenchman to win Roland-Garros since 1946.

#27

ILIE NASTASE, "NASTY"

BORN JULY 19, 1946 IN BUCHAREST, ROMANIA.

Ilie Năstase won two Grand Slam singles titles: the US Open in 1972 and the French Open in 1973. Năstase was also a finalist at Wimbledon and the Australian Open. He was the first player ranked world number one when the ATP introduced computerized rankings in 1973.

THE DUALITY OF NĂSTASE

Ilie Năstase is famous for his incredible on-court talent and often controversial behavior. His flamboyant personality and spectacular playing style attracted many fans, but his volatile temper and on-court outbursts also drew criticism. Năstase was a true showman, bringing both artistry and drama to tennis. His influence extends beyond his victories, having helped increase popularity and entertainment in the sport.

Năstase's career was punctuated by memorable moments, including his victory at the US Open in 1972, where he demonstrated his technical superiority, and his triumph at Roland Garros in 1973. His confrontations with contemporaries like Bjorn Borg and John McEnroe became a tennis legend for their intensity and spectacle. Off the court, Năstase is known for his charisma and media presence, having maintained a high popularity well after his professional career ended.

Ilie Năstase was the first professional athlete to sign a contract with Nike in 1972.

#28

JOHN NEWCOMBE, "NEWK"

BORN MAY 23, 1944 IN SYDNEY, AUSTRALIA.

John Newcombe won 7 Grand Slam singles titles, including three at Wimbledon (1967, 1970, 1971) and two at the US Open (1973, 1975), as well as two titles at the Australian Open (1973, 1975). Newcombe also excelled in doubles, winning 17 Grand Slam titles.

STRENGTH AND FINESSE

John Newcombe is famous for his dynamic playing style and charismatic on-court personality. He was recognized for his ability to combine power and finesse, particularly effective on grass. His dominance at Wimbledon and his performances in the Davis Cup, where he helped Australia win numerous titles, made tennis history. Newcombe was also a pioneer in the Open era, adapting his game for success on both the amateur and professional circuits.

Highlights of Newcombe's career include his victories at Wimbledon, where he demonstrated his mastery of the grass court game. His duels with contemporaries like Rod Laver and Ken Rosewall were career highlights. Off the court, Newcombe has been an ambassador for tennis, contributing to the sport's popularity in Australia and around the world. His transition into the role of coach and commentator has also been an important part of his tennis legacy.

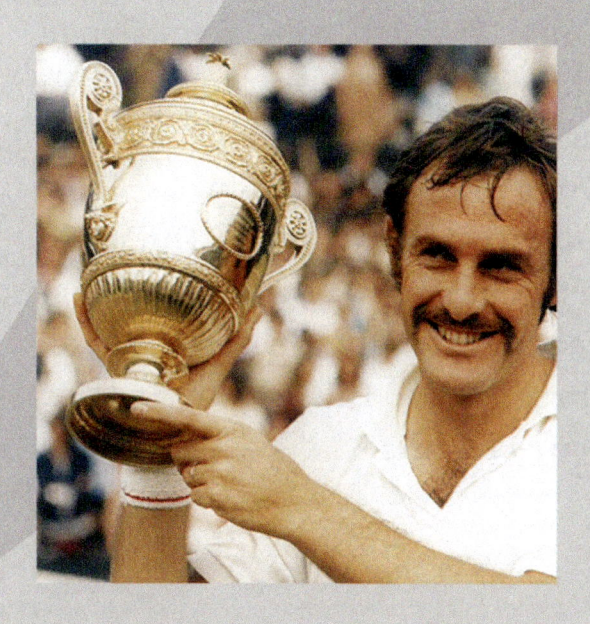

John Newcombe was nicknamed "Newk" due to the difficulty some commentators had in pronouncing his surname correctly.

#29

TONY TRABERT

BORN AUGUST 16, 1930 IN CINCINNATI, OHIO, UNITED STATES.

Tony Trabert won five Grand Slam singles titles: the US Open in 1953 and 1955, the French Open and Wimbledon in 1955, and the Australian Open in 1955. 1955 was a phenomenal year for Trabert, where he won three of the four major tournaments.

COURT DOMINATOR OF THE 50S

Tony Trabert is famous for being one of the most dominant players in world tennis during the 1950s. His exceptional season in 1955, where he won the majority of Grand Slam tournaments, remains a career highlight. Trabert is known for his versatility on different types of courts, his impeccable technique and his ability to execute powerful shots.

Trabert's career was marked by several significant moments, especially his year 1955. His consecutive victories in major tournaments testify to his supremacy during that era. Off the court, Trabert also made a significant impact as a coach and commentator, helping to popularize tennis in the United States. His transition from gaming to sports journalism and administration showed his passion and commitment to the sport.

He is one of two American players, along with Art Larsen, who managed to win the United States championships on four different surfaces.

#30

MARIA SHARAPOVA, "MASHA"

BORN APRIL 19, 1987 IN NYAGAN, RUSSIA.

Maria Sharapova has enjoyed a career marked by five major singles titles, including two victories at Wimbledon in 2004 and 2006, a victory at the US Open in 2006, and two titles at Roland Garros in 2012 and 2014. She also won a total of 36 singles titles on the WTA Tour, reaching the top of the world rankings in 2005.

THE RUSSIAN ICON IN POWERFUL SERVICE

Maria Sharapova is famous for her incredible work ethic, determination and intensity on the court. Her victory at Wimbledon at the age of 17 catapulted her into the spotlight, and she remained a dominant force in women's tennis for many years. Aside from her athletic prowess, Sharapova is also known for her business acumen, having built a successful personal brand and being involved in various ventures.

Sharapova's career has been punctuated by memorable moments, such as her first Grand Slam victory at Wimbledon, beating Serena Williams in the final. His triumphs at Roland Garros, completing the Career Grand Slam, attest to his versatility on different surfaces. Her career was also marked by injuries and controversies, including a suspension for doping, after which she made a notable return to the circuit.

On June 8, 2016, Maria Sharapova was suspended for two years by the International Tennis Federation, after having tested positive for meldonium in January, during the Australian Open, suspension finally reduced to fifteen months after an appeal made to the Court of Arbitration for Sport which declares that she did not consume a doping product voluntarily and in a minimal quantity.

#31

PANCHO SEGURA, "LITTLE PANCHO"

BORN JUNE 20, 1921 IN GUAYAQUIL, ECUADOR.

Pancho Segura may not have won any Grand Slam singles titles, but he remains one of the most influential and talented players of the amateur and professional tennis era of the 1940s and 1950s. He won several major titles on the professional circuit, including the United States Pro Championship three times.

TWO-HANDED FOREHAND MASTER

Pancho Segura is famous for popularizing the two-handed forehand, a technique that has become a common feature in modern tennis. His small size and robust build did not prevent him from competing with the best players of his era. His style of play, characterized by agility, speed and impeccable technique, defied the conventions of the time. He was also known for his warm personality and charisma.

Segura's career was marked by his victories in professional tournaments, where he faced and beat some of the best tennis players. His matches against legends like Pancho Gonzales and Jack Kramer have gone down in history as examples of exceptional competitiveness and talent. After his playing career, Segura was an influential coach, mentoring players like Jimmy Connors, and helping to shape future generations of tennis champions.

Pancho Segura has been a member of the International Tennis Hall of Fame since 1984.

#32

MANUEL SANTANA, "MANOLO"

BORN MAY 10, 1938 IN MADRID, SPAIN.

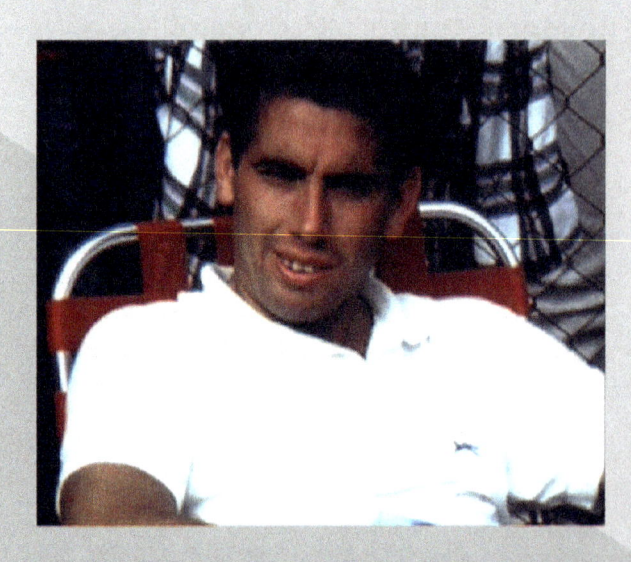

Manuel Santana is an emblematic figure of Spanish tennis. He won four Grand Slam singles titles: Roland Garros in 1961 and 1964, the US Open in 1965 and Wimbledon in 1966. These victories were particularly significant, marking Spain's entry onto the tennis scene. global.

THE PIONEER OF SPANISH TENNIS

Manuel Santana is famous for being one of the first Spanish tennis players to achieve international success. His victory at Wimbledon in 1966 was a historic moment, as he was one of the first clay court tennis players to triumph on the grass court at Wimbledon. His versatile style of play, his elegance on the court and his ability to excel on different surfaces have made him a legend in tennis.

Santana's career has been punctuated by many highlights, including his two victories at Roland Garros and his historic triumph at Wimbledon. He also played a key role in the Spanish team's Davis Cup success. After his retirement, Santana continued to influence tennis, notably as tournament director in Madrid, contributing to the growth and popularization of tennis in Spain.

He accidentally becomes a ball boy at the Velasquez Tenis Club in Madrid in order to earn money for his family. Having left school at the age of ten, he spent most of his time kicking balls with other young people his age in the same club.

#33

JIM COURIER, "BIG JIM."

BORN ON AUGUST 17, 1970 IN SANFORD, FLORIDA, USA.

Jim Courier is a former American professional tennis player, particularly active in the 1990s. He won four Grand Slam singles titles: twice the Australian Open (1992, 1993) and twice Roland-Garros (1991). , 1992). Courier was also world number one, a rank he held for 58 weeks.

POWER AND PERSEVERANCE

Jim Courier is famous for his aggressive playing style and great physical ability. He was known for his hitting power, particularly his forehand, and his endurance on court, allowing him to prevail in long and grueling matches. Courier was also renowned for his rigorous mental approach to the game, focusing intensely on each game. His consecutive double victory at the Australian Open and French Open was a notable achievement, placing him among the best players of his generation.

Courier's career was punctuated by several notable moments, including his Grand Slam victories, which highlighted his ability to excel on different surfaces. His performance at Roland Garros, where he won two consecutive titles, was particularly impressive. Off the court, Courier is also recognized for his work as a tennis commentator, offering insightful analysis and sharing his expertise of the game.

Jim Courier began playing tennis in the 1980s and joined Nick Bollettieri's academy, where he rubbed shoulders with other future champions, such as Andre Agassi or Monica Seles.

#34

PATRICK RAFTER, "PAT"

BORN DECEMBER 28, 1972 IN MOUNT ISA, QUEENSLAND, AUSTRALIA.

Patrick Rafter won two Grand Slam singles titles, both at the US Open in 1997 and 1998. Rafter was also a finalist at Wimbledon in 2000 and 2001. Known for his impeccable volleying and strong serve, Rafter was the one of the last serve-volley specialists in men's tennis.

THE CHARISMATIC AUSTRALIAN OF TENNIS

Patrick Rafter is famous for his dynamic playing style, charismatic personality and fair play on the court. His aggressive serve-and-volley approach distinguished him in an era where the baseline game began to dominate. Rafter was well-liked by fans for his sportsmanlike demeanor and humble attitude, as much as for his on-court performances. He was a role model for young players and contributed greatly to the popularity of tennis in Australia.

Rafter's career was highlighted by his back-to-back US Open victories, putting him in the international spotlight. His finals at Wimbledon against Pete Sampras and Goran Ivanišević remain classic matches, showing his ability to compete with the best players on grass. Off the court, Rafter is known for his philanthropic efforts and commitment to various charitable causes.

Pat Rafter began to make a name for himself in 1993 by eliminating world No. 1 Pete Sampras at the Indianapolis tournament, when he was only ranked 139th in the world.

#35

THOMAS MUSTER, "THE LIZARD"

BORN OCTOBER 2, 1967 IN LEIBNITZ, AUSTRIA.

Thomas Muster recognized for his mastery on clay, won the French Open in 1995, his only Grand Slam title, but also accumulated an impressive total of 44 career titles, most of them on clay. Muster reached number one in the world in 1996.

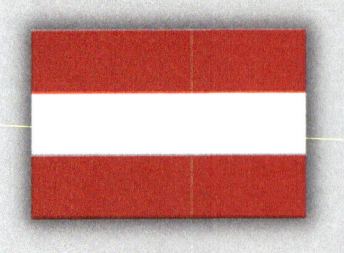

THE MASTER OF CLAY

Thomas Muster is famous for his incredible resilience and dominance on clay in the 1990s. He made a remarkable comeback after a serious car accident in 1989, which nearly ended his career. Muster has become a symbol of determination and mental strength, overcoming obstacles to reach the heights of tennis. His ability to maintain a high level of play during long rallies on clay has been a key element of his success.

Muster's career was marked by several memorable moments, including his victory at the French Open in 1995, which crowned his career. His series of victories on clay, particularly in 1995 when he won a record number of titles on this surface, remains a remarkable achievement. Off the court, Muster is recognized for his contribution to Austrian tennis, having greatly increased the popularity of the sport in his native country.

He holds the record of twenty-six titles in the ATP 250 Series category. He is the third player in the Open era to have won the most titles on clay.

#36

LLEYTON HEWITT, "RUSTY"

BORN FEBRUARY 24, 1981 IN ADELAIDE, AUSTRALIA.

Lleyton Hewitt won two Grand Slam singles titles: the US Open in 2001 and Wimbledon in 2002. Hewitt was also a runner-up at the Australian Open in 2005. He reached the world No. 1 ranking in 2001, becoming the youngest male player to do so at the age of 20.

THE LION-HEARTED AUSTRALIAN WARRIOR

Lleyton Hewitt is famous for his fighting spirit and relentless approach to tennis. He left his mark on Australian tennis with his exceptional performances, including his victory at Wimbledon in 2002. His on-court charisma and determination made him a crowd favorite and an icon of Australian tennis.

In addition to his Grand Slam success, Hewitt was a mainstay of the Australian Davis Cup team. He helped Australia win the Davis Cup in 1999 and 2003, cementing his reputation as an exceptional leader and competitor.

Hewitt was also known for his exciting rivalry with other great players of his era, such as Andre Agassi, Andy Roddick and Roger Federer. His epic on-court duels have captivated fans around the world.

Lleyton Hewitt participated in his first Grand Slam tournament in Australia in 1997 at just 15 years old. The youngest player in the history of the tournament to come out of qualifying, he was eliminated in the first round by Sergi Bruguera.

#37

ANDY RODDICK, "A-ROD"

BORN AUGUST 30, 1982 IN OMAHA, NEBRASKA, UNITED STATES.

Andy Roddick has won a total of 32 singles titles on the ATP Tour, including a major title at the US Open in 2003. He also reached No. 1 in the world singles rankings in 2003 and finished the year as as world number one. Roddick was a key member of the U.S. Davis Cup team, contributing to the team's victory in 2007.

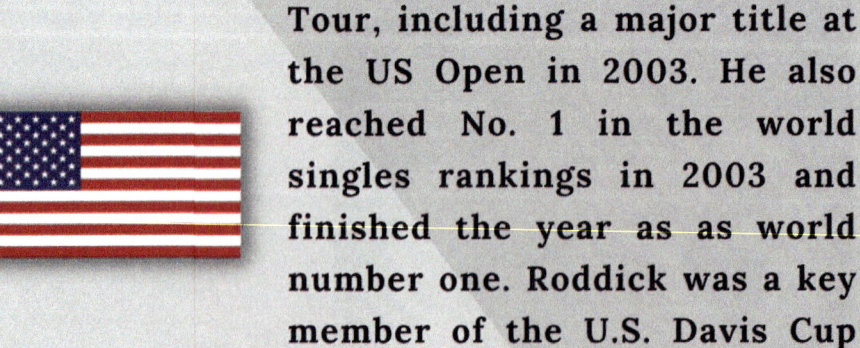

THE MASTER OF LIGHTNING SERVICE

Lleyton Hewitt is famous for his exceptional fighting spirit and competitive spirit. His victory at Wimbledon in 2002 was a highlight of his career, making him history as one of the tournament's youngest winners. Hewitt was also known for his battle cry "Come on!" on the court, symbolizing his combative attitude and determination.

Hewitt's career was marked by his Grand Slam victories and his position as world number one. His matches against players like Roger Federer, Rafael Nadal and Andy Roddick were remembered for their intensity. Off the court, Hewitt has been recognized for his involvement in the Davis Cup, leading the Australian team to several successes. His transition to the role of Davis Cup captain following his retirement showed his continued commitment to Australian tennis.

Andy Roddick is often called "the other A-Rod" in reference to baseball star Alex Rodriguez who already had this nickname. In Texas, the state where he is from

#38

TONY ROCHE, "ROCKET"

BORN MAY 17, 1945 IN TARCUTTA, NEW SOUTH WALES, AUSTRALIA.

Tony Roche won a Grand Slam singles title at the French Open in 1966 and was runner-up at several other major tournaments, including Wimbledon and the US Open. In doubles, Roche excelled, winning 13 Grand Slam titles, often partnering compatriot John Newcombe.

MASTER OF THE FLY AND MENTOR

Tony Roche is famous for his mastery of volleying, an essential skill in tennis of his era. His aggressive style of play and ability to play well on all surfaces have earned him a place among the tennis greats. After his playing career, Roche became an influential coach, guiding players like Ivan Lendl and Roger Federer. His contribution to tennis as a player and coach has been immense, influencing generations of players.

Roche's career was marked by his victory at Roland Garros and his doubles successes, particularly at Wimbledon and the US Open. His Grand Slam singles finals against the likes of Rod Laver and Ken Rosewall remain memorable moments. As a coach, his influence on the play and technique of legendary players like Lendl and Federer was significant, leaving a lasting imprint on the sport.

He subsequently enjoyed a legendary coaching career, notably coaching three world No. 1s, helping them win numerous major titles.

#39

FRED STOLLE, "THE FOX"

BORN OCTOBER 8, 1938 IN HORNSBY, NEW SOUTH WALES, AUSTRALIA.

Fred Stolle won two Grand Slam singles titles: the US Open in 1966 and the French Open in 1965. In doubles, he was exceptional, winning 10 Grand Slam titles, often partnering Roy Emerson. Stolle was renowned for his powerful serve, volleying game and ability to excel on grass.

A KEY FIGURE IN AUSTRALIAN TENNIS

Fred Stolle is famous for being a central part of the golden era of Australian tennis. His versatility on different surfaces and his success in doubles are particularly notable. Stolle was a key member of the Australian Davis Cup team, contributing to several victories for his country in this competition. His dynamic game, combined with his sportsmanship, has made him a respected figure in the world of tennis.

Stolle's career has been punctuated by notable moments, including his Grand Slam victories and his Davis Cup successes. His doubles performances alongside Roy Emerson have gone down in history as some of the best in tennis. After his retirement, Stolle became a respected coach and commentator, contributing to the evolution of tennis well beyond his playing career.

Fred Stolle has been a member of the International Tennis Hall of Fame since 1985

#40

JACK CRAWFORD
"GENTLEMAN JACK"

BORN MARCH 22, 1908 IN ALBURY, NEW SOUTH WALES, AUSTRALIA.

Jack Crawford won six Grand Slam singles titles: the Australian Open three times (1931, 1932, 1935), French Open in 1933, Wimbledon in 1933 and the US Open in 1933. His year 1933 was particularly remarkable, because he narrowly missed achieving a calendar Grand Slam, a feat rarely approached at the time.

THE AUSTRALIAN TENNIS ACE OF THE 1930S

Jack Crawford is famous for his grace and elegance both on and off the court. He was one of the first players to excel on all surfaces, demonstrating remarkable versatility. His near-successful attempt at a calendar Grand Slam in 1933 remains one of the most memorable moments in tennis history. Crawford was also known for his gentlemanly demeanor, earning the respect and admiration of fans and players.

The most notable moments of Crawford's career include his Grand Slam victories, particularly the year 1933, which set a standard of success and consistency. His duels with players like Fred Perry and Ellsworth Vines have gone down in history as examples of competition at its finest. Crawford also played an important role in Australia's Davis Cup successes.

He was the husband of the player Marjorie Cox Crawford, with whom he won three consecutive times in mixed doubles at the Australian Open, between 1931 and 1933.

#41

BILLIE JEAN KING, "BJK"

BORN NOVEMBER 22, 1943 IN LONG BEACH, CALIFORNIA, UNITED STATES.

Billie Jean King has won an impressive total of 39 Grand Slam titles, including 12 in singles, 16 in women's doubles and 11 in mixed doubles. His major victories include 6 Wimbledon singles titles. King was ranked world number one several times during the 1960s and 1970s.

A PIONEER ON AND OFF THE COURT

Billie Jean King is famous not only for her sporting successes, but also for her pioneering role in the fight for gender equality in sports. Her match against Bobby Riggs in 1973, known as the "Battle of the Sexes", was a significant cultural moment and contributed greatly to the recognition of women's tennis. King also played a crucial role in the founding of the Women's Tennis Association (WTA) and was a strong advocate for players' rights.

Besides her legendary "Battle of the Sexes", notable moments in King's career include her multiple victories at Wimbledon and the US Open, which demonstrated her dominance in women's tennis. Her commitment to gender equality and her efforts to promote women's tennis have left an indelible mark on the history of the sport. Off the court, his activism and leadership have been a global source of inspiration.

King is equally known for her commitment to gender equality and the recognition of women's sports. Very active during her career, she founded the Women's Tennis Association (WTA) in 1973, of which she became its first president. In September 2020, the Fed Cup was renamed in his name.

#42

MONICA SELES

BORN DECEMBER 2, 1973 IN NOVI SAD, YUGOSLAVIA (NOW SERBIA).

Before turning 20, Monica Seles had already won nine Grand Slam titles, including four Australian Opens (1991-1993, 1996), three Roland-Garros (1990-1992) and two US Opens (1991, 1992). Known for her powerful baseline game and famous moan, Seles was the youngest world number one in women's tennis history at the time.

EARLY TALENT

Monica Seles is famous for her ability to dominate her opponents with offensive play and double striking from both ends. His rivalry with Steffi Graf was one of the most intense in tennis history. Her career was tragically cut short in 1993 when she was stabbed during a match, an event that not only marked her career but also had a profound impact on the world of tennis. His ability to return to the highest level after this attack is a testament to his mental strength and resilience.

Aside from her Grand Slam victories, notable moments in Seles' career include her return to tennis in 1995 following her assault, where she quickly regained a place among the elite of women's tennis. His victory at the Australian Open in 1996, after his return, was particularly emotional and demonstrated his incredible competitive spirit.

Her hunt for records came to an abrupt end in April 1993 when, in the middle of a match in Hamburg, a 38-year-old German worker stabbed her in the back.

#43

DAVID NALBANDIAN "KING DAVID"

BORN JANUARY 1, 1982 IN CÓRDOBA, ARGENTINA.

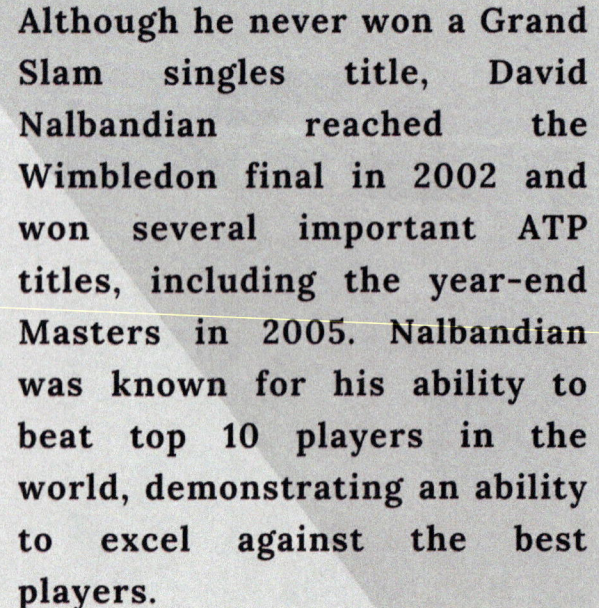

Although he never won a Grand Slam singles title, David Nalbandian reached the Wimbledon final in 2002 and won several important ATP titles, including the year-end Masters in 2005. Nalbandian was known for his ability to beat top 10 players in the world, demonstrating an ability to excel against the best players.

THE CHALLENGE TO THE GIANTS OF TENNIS

Nalbandian is famous for his all-around playing style and versatility. He was able to play effectively on all surfaces, which allowed him to compete with the best players of his era. His tactical intelligence, powerful forehand and two-handed backhand were key elements of his success. Nalbandian was also renowned for his spectacular comebacks and his ability to remain calm in critical moments.

Notable moments in Nalbandian's career include his victory at the 2005 Masters, where he beat several top players, and his final at Wimbledon. His victory at the Paris Masters in 2007, where he beat three consecutive world number one ranked players (Roger Federer, Rafael Nadal and Novak Djokovic), remains a rare feat in tennis history. Nalbandian was also a key member of Argentina's Davis Cup team, contributing to several important victories.

He is the only player in history to achieve the feat of beating Novak Djokovic, Roger Federer and Rafael Nadal in the same tournament during the Madrid Tennis Tournament (ATP 2007).

#44

MARTINA NAVRATILOVA

BORN OCTOBER 18, 1956 IN PRAGUE, CZECHOSLOVAKIA, LATER TOOK AMERICAN CITIZENSHIP.

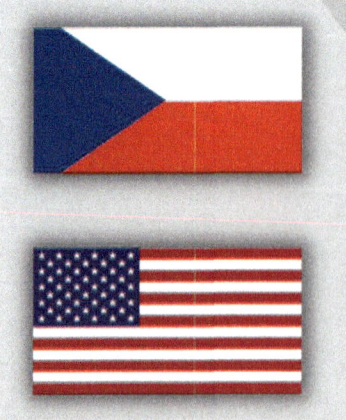

Martina Navratilova has won 18 Grand Slam singles titles, including 9 at Wimbledon, a record for a woman in the Open era. Her 31 Grand Slam titles in women's doubles and 10 in mixed doubles. Navratilova was world number one in singles for an impressive total of 332 weeks and in doubles for 237 weeks.

THE UNDISPUTED SUPREMACY OF NAVRATILOVA

Martina Navratilova transformed tennis into a sport rising beyond the standards of her time. Navratilova also made history as one of the first openly gay athletes, playing a key role in advancing the visibility and acceptance of LGBTQ+ athletes in professional sports. Her statistics, notably her 167 singles and 177 doubles titles, remain records in women's tennis, testifying to her supremacy and indelible impact on the sport.

Martina Navratilova is not only a tennis icon for her on-court exploits, but also for her influence off it. In 1975, facing oppression in her native Czechoslovakia, she made the bold choice to seek political asylum in the United States, a courageous act that marked the beginning of a new era in her life and her life. career. Her commitment to the rights of women and the LGBTQ+ community has made her a leading figure in the fights for equality and social justice. On the court, his ability to adapt and excel on all playing surfaces is remarkable, winning major titles on grass, clay and hard courts. She also defied norms of sporting longevity, winning major titles well into her 40s, proving that age and performance are not necessarily linked.

Her rivalry with Chris Evert, seen as one of the greatest in the history of the game, enlivened the women's circuit during the 1970s and 1980s.

#45

VENUS WILLIAMS

BORN JUNE 17, 1980 IN LYNWOOD, CALIFORNIA, UNITED STATES.

Venus Williams has won 7 Grand Slam singles titles, including 5 at Wimbledon, demonstrating impressive mastery on grass. In doubles, she shone alongside her sister Serena Williams, winning 14 Grand Slam titles. Venus also won four Olympic gold medals, including one in singles and three in doubles.

THE TRIUMPHAL ASCENSION

Venus Williams is famous not only for her titles and performances on the court, but also for breaking barriers in a sport traditionally dominated by non-black athletes. Her rivalry with her sister Serena has captivated fans around the world. Venus also played a key role in the evolution of pay parity in tennis, particularly at Wimbledon, where she was a driving force for equal pay for men and women.

In 2000, she achieved a rare feat by winning both Wimbledon and the US Open, launching an era of dominance that lasted several years. Her victory at Wimbledon in 2005, after a period of injuries and fluctuating form, was a testament to her resilience. Venus has also been a role model for young black athletes, paving the way for greater diversity in sports. Off the court, she is recognized for her involvement in various social causes and her fashion business, which combines her love for design with her business acumen. Despite her diagnosis with Sjögren's syndrome, an autoimmune disease, she continued to compete at the highest level, illustrating uncommon strength of character and determination.

She holds the absolute record (men and women combined) for the number of participations in the main draw of the four Grand Slam tournaments, with 91 participations, as well as the absolute record for the number of participations in the main draw of Roland-Garros, with 24 participations between 1997 and 2021.

#46

ROY EMERSON, "EMMO"

BORN NOVEMBER 3, 1936 IN BLACKBUTT, QUEENSLAND, AUSTRALIA

Roy Emerson won a total of 12 Grand Slam singles titles, including 6 at the Australian Open, a record for his era. His successes are not limited to the simple ones; he also won 16 Grand Slam doubles titles. Emerson is the first player in history to win every singles and doubles Grand Slam.

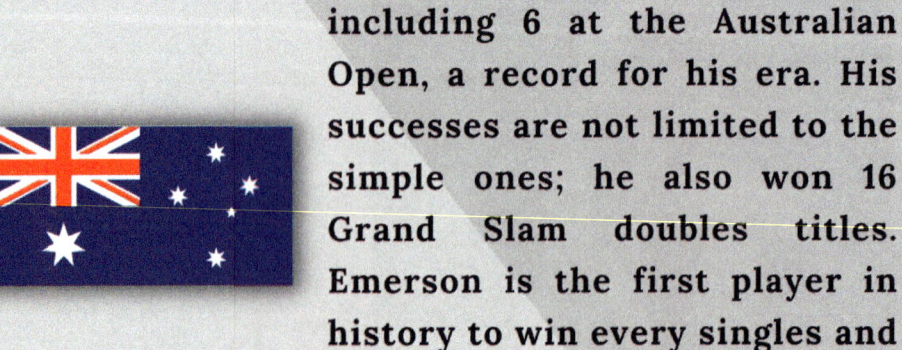

UNDISPUTED MASTER OF THE 1960S

His versatile style of play, combining power and finesse, allowed him to dominate on all surfaces, a rarity in his era. Emerson is also recognized for his remarkable physical condition and his ability to maintain a high level of performance over long and grueling matches. His 12 Grand Slam singles titles, a record until the modern era, as well as his 16 doubles titles, attest to his supremacy in both formats.

One of the most remarkable aspects of Emerson's career is its longevity and consistency. He maintained his status among tennis' elite well past the age when many of his contemporaries had retired. His impact extends beyond his Grand Slam victories. Emerson was a key member of the Australian Davis Cup team, contributing to several victories for his country in this prestigious competition. Additionally, he played a crucial role in the transition from amateur to professional tennis, paving the way for future generations. His humble personality and unwavering work ethic have also made him a role model for young players and a respected ambassador for the sport.

For 13 consecutive years (from 1959 to 1971) he was winner or finalist of at least 1 Grand Slam tournament, always in singles and doubles combined (another record).

#47

STEFFI GRAF "FRAULEIN FOREHAND"

BORN JUNE 14, 1969 IN MANNHEIM, GERMANY.

Her record includes 22 Grand Slam singles titles, the second highest total in the Open era for women. Steffi Graf achieved the "Golden Slam" in 1988, winning all four major tournaments and the Olympic gold medal that same year. Graf was also world number one for a record 377 weeks.

GRAF'S GOLDEN ERA

Steffi Graf is famous for her unprecedented dominance in women's tennis. His ability to adapt to all surfaces, combined with his aggressive play and famous forehand stroke, defined a new era in the sport. Perhaps the most notable achievement of her career was the 1988 "Golden Slam", where she not only won all the Grand Slam titles, but also the gold medal at the Seoul Olympics. This feat underlines his exceptional talent and his superiority in the world of tennis.

Beyond his Grand Slam titles, Graf left his mark on tennis with his consistency and longevity. She finished eight consecutive years as world number one, a record that speaks to her dominance. Her rapid adaptation from promising junior to world champion was meteoric, winning her first Grand Slam at the age of 17 at Roland Garros. His game has evolved over the years, demonstrating a remarkable ability to overcome varied opponents and playing styles. Off the court, Graf has been recognized for her involvement in charitable causes, using her fame to positively influence society. Even after her retirement, her legacy continues to inspire new generations of players.

She is the longest-serving player in the world, holding the record for eight completed seasons and 377 cumulative weeks – including 186 consecutive weeks, tied with Serena Williams.

#48

MARGARET COURT

BORN JULY 16, 1942 IN ALBURY, NEW SOUTH WALES, AUSTRALIA.

Margaret Court holds the record for 24 Grand Slam singles titles. His talent was not limited to the simple ones; she also won 19 Grand Slam doubles titles and 21 mixed doubles titles, totaling 64 major titles. Court achieved the singles Grand Slam in 1970, winning all four majors that same year.

A BREATHTAKING TRACK RECORD

Her unique combination of power, agility and technique has propelled her to the top of world tennis. The most remarkable achievement of her career remains her Grand Slam in 1970, where she triumphed in all major tournaments, asserting her undisputed superiority. Her ability to maintain a high level of performance over a long period of time, including after becoming a mother, broke stereotypes about female athletes and their careers.

Margaret Court not only dominated women's tennis for a decade, but was also a pioneer in several aspects. His adaptation to professional tennis in the 1960s was remarkable, dominating the scene at a time when the sport was undergoing major changes. She was renowned for her intensive physical training, a less common practice at the time, which gave her an advantage over her opponents. Her post-motherhood career is particularly impressive; she continued to win major titles after the birth of her children, demonstrating an incredible ability to balance family life and high-level sport. Off the court, his opinions and positions have often sparked controversy, which has contributed to his notoriety well beyond tennis.

She has been a member of the International Tennis Hall of Fame since 1979.

#49

LEW HOAD, "THE BLOND BOMBER"

BORN 23 NOVEMBER 1934 IN GLEBE, AUSTRALIA.

Lew Hoad has won four Grand Slam singles titles, including the Australian Open twice, Wimbledon once and the US Open once. Hoad also shone in doubles, winning 13 Grand Slam titles, often partnering compatriot and rival Ken Rosewall.

THE EXPLOSIVE IMPACT OF LEW HOAD

His powerful serve and groundstrokes, often described as revolutionary for the time, laid the foundations of modern tennis. Hoad was known for his intense rivalry with Ken Rosewall, providing the tennis world with some of the most memorable confrontations in history. He was also recognized for his ability to play exceptionally under pressure, often coming back from difficult situations to win.

One of the most notable moments of Hoad's career was 1956, when he was in contention to achieve the Grand Slam in singles, a rare feat. Although he was ultimately unsuccessful, his performance that year remains one of the most impressive in tennis history. In addition to his singles exploits, his doubles career with Rosewall is legendary, the two forming one of the most formidable pairs of their era. Hoad was also known for his resilience in the face of injury, often playing and winning despite physical pain. After retiring from professional tennis, he continued to influence the sport as a coach and commentator, sharing his passion and deep knowledge of the game.

Lew Hoad was the first player to use a metal racket at the Australian Open in 1957. This innovation aroused the curiosity and admiration of tennis fans, marking an important step in the evolution of tennis equipment. tennis.

#50

CHRIS EVERT, "ICE MAIDEN"

BORN DECEMBER 21, 1954 IN FORT LAUDERDALE, FLORIDA, UNITED STATES.

With 18 Grand Slam singles titles to her credit, her career is dotted with triumphs, notably at Roland Garros where she won seven titles. Evert was the world number one for 260 weeks. His consistency in Grand Slams is legendary, with a series of 34 consecutive semi-finals.

FROZEN PRECISION

Chris Evert is famous for his imperturbable calm and surgical precision on the court, earning him the nickname "Ice Maiden". Her game, characterized by precise groundstrokes and a mental steel, redefined women's tennis. Her rivalry with Navratilova was not only a clash of styles, but also a struggle for supremacy in women's tennis, producing unforgettable matches. Evert transformed the two-handed backhand into a fearsome weapon, influencing generations of players.

Chris Evert's career is punctuated by defining moments, going beyond his Grand Slam victories. She maintained an impressive winning percentage of over 90% for most of her career, a record in the sport. His streak of 125 consecutive victories on clay between 1973 and 1979 is a testimony to his mastery on this surface. Evert also played a key role in popularizing women's tennis in the 1970s and 1980s, attracting a new audience to the sport. Outside of tennis, she has been active in various charitable causes and has been a respected sports commentator, continuing to contribute to the tennis world well after her retirement.

In January 2022, Chris Evert revealed that she had ovarian cancer. Her younger sister Jeanne, also suffering from the same illness and died in February 2020, is "a source of inspiration to help overcome this ordeal", according to her

At the close of "The 50 Legends of Tennis and Their Stories", we salute these exceptional players who have written the pages of this extraordinary sport. Their victories, defeats, sacrifices and moments of grace have made tennis a symbol of determination and fair play.

Each of these champions embodies the spirit of tennis, a blend of competition, respect and elegance.

These tennis legends will continue to inspire future generations to pursue their dreams, persevere in the face of adversity and strive for excellence. Their legacy lives on on courts around the world, reminding everyone that effort and passion are the keys to success.
are the keys to success.

Printed in Great Britain
by Amazon